Henry D. Thoreau.

HENRY DAVID THOREAU
(1817—1862)

QUOTATIONS

OF

Henry David Thoreau

APPLEWOOD BOOKS
Carlisle, Massachusetts

Henry David Thoreau

HENRY DAVID THOREAU was born on July 12, 1817, at his grandmother's farmhouse in Concord, Massachusetts, the third of four children to John and Cynthia Thoreau. As a child he attended the public schools of Concord, then went to Harvard College in 1834 and graduated in 1837 when he was twenty years old. He was hired as the teacher of the Center School in Concord but resigned after two weeks because of a dispute over corporal punishment. At odds about how to earn a living, he unhappily went to work for his father, who was a pencil maker.

In 1841 Thoreau went to live in the home of his mentor and friend, Ralph Waldo Emerson, whom he'd met in 1837. It was because of Emerson that Thoreau became deeply involved with the Transcendentalists and befriended many of the leading thinkers and writers of the day, including Bronson Alcott, Margaret Fuller, and Nathaniel Hawthorne. At Emerson's urging Thoreau began to keep a journal, and it became an almost daily habit for Thoreau to write in it; by the time of his death it consisted of over 2 million words.

In 1845 Emerson allowed Thoreau to build a house on some land that Emerson owned near Walden Pond in Concord. Thoreau built a small one-room house there, moving in on July 4, 1845. He went to Walden to write his first book, *A Week on the Concord and Merrimack Rivers*, and to conduct an "experiment" in simple living. He would stay at Walden Pond for two years, two months, and two days. It was in 1846 that Thoreau spent one night in jail for not paying the Massachusetts poll tax, an incident that inspired his essay "Resistance to Civil Government," first published in 1849 and later known as "Civil Disobedience" after his death.

Thoreau published just two books in his lifetime: *A Week on the Concord and Merrimack Rivers* in 1849 and *Walden; or, Life in the Woods* in 1854. The first sold poorly, while *Walden* was modestly more successful. Neither book made him famous or wealthy.

Thoreau was an outspoken abolitionist, and he helped escaped slaves make their way to Canada on the Underground Railroad. In 1854 he delivered "Slavery in Massachusetts," an attack on the Fugitive Slave Law. He met the radical abolitionist John Brown in 1857 and publicly supported Brown's raid on the federal arsenal at Harpers Ferry, Virginia, in 1859.

The last years of Thoreau's life were spent in studying, journaling, and lecturing on the natural phenomena of his native town. He died of tuberculosis on May 6, 1862, at the family home on Main Street in Concord. He was forty-four years old.

QUOTATIONS

OF

Henry David
Thoreau

*T*o be alone I find it necessary to escape the present — I avoid myself...I seek a garret. The spiders must not be disturbed, nor the floors swept, nor the lumber arranged.

– Thoreau's *Journal*, October 22, 1837

Henry D. Thoreau

*T*ruth strikes us from behind, and in the dark, as well as from before and in broad day-light.

– Thoreau's *Journal*, November 5, 1837

Henry D. Thoreau

*T*he human soul is a silent harp in God's quire, whose strings need only to be swept by the divine breath to chime in with the harmonies of creation.

– Thoreau's *Journal*, August 10, 1838

Henry D. Thoreau

*T*here is no remedy for love but to love more.

– Thoreau's *Journal*, July 25, 1839

Henry D. Thoreau

*N*ature will bear the closest inspection. She invites us to lay our eye level with her smallest leaf, and take an insect view of its plain.

– Thoreau's *Journal*, October 22, 1839

*T*here is as much music in the world as virtue. In a world of peace and love music would be the universal language.... It is the herald of virtue. It is God's voice.

– *"The Service,"* 1840

*O*n the death of a friend, we should consider that the fates through confidence have devolved on us the task of a double living, that we have henceforth to fulfill the promise of our friend's life also.

– Thoreau's *Journal*, February 28, 1840

*A*n early morning walk is a blessing for the whole day.

– Thoreau's *Journal*, April 20, 1840

*G*reat thoughts make great men. Without these no heraldry nor blood will avail.

– Thoreau's *Journal*, February 7, 1841

*M*y life is the poem I would have writ, but I could not both live and utter it.
– Thoreau's *Journal*, August 28, 1841

I think I could write a poem to be called Concord.... For argument I should have the River — the Woods — the Ponds — the Hills — the Fields — the Swamps and Meadows — the Streets and Buildings — and the Villagers. Then Morning — Noon — and Evening — Spring — Autumn and Winter — Night-Indian Summer — and the Mountains in the Horizon.
– Thoreau's *Journal*, September 4, 1841

I want to go soon and live away by the pond where I shall hear only the wind whispering among the reeds. It will be success if I have left myself behind. But my friends ask what will I do when I get there. Will it not be employment enough to watch the progress of the seasons?
– Thoreau's *Journal*, December 24, 1841

*N*ature is mythical and mystical always, and works with the license and extravagance of genius. She has her luxurious and florid style as well as art.
– *"Natural History of Massachusetts,"* 1842

Henry D Thoreau

*I*n society you will not find health, but in nature. Unless our feet at least stood in the midst of nature, all our faces would be pale and livid.
– *"Natural History of Massachusetts,"* 1842

Henry D Thoreau

*T*hose authors are successful who do not write down to others, but make their own taste and judgment their audience. It is enough if I please myself with writing; I am then sure of an audience.
– Thoreau's *Journal*, March 24, 1842

Henry D Thoreau

*H*ow meanly and grossly do we deal with nature! Can we not do more than cut and trim the forest?
– *"Paradise (to Be) Regained,"* 1843

I don't like [New York] city better the more I see it, but worse. I am ashamed of my eyes that I behold it. It is a thousand times meaner than I could have imagined.... The pigs in the street are the most respectable portion of the population. When will the world learn that a million men are of no importance compared with one man?
– From a letter to Ralph Waldo Emerson, June 8, 1843

Henry D Thoreau

I wish to meet the facts of life — the vital facts, which are the phenomenon or actuality the gods meant to show us — face to face, and so I came down [to Walden Pond]. Life! Who knows what it is, what it does? If I am not quite right here, I am less wrong than before.
– Thoreau's *Journal*, July 6, 1845

Henry D Thoreau

*T*here can be no really black melon-cholly [*sic*] to him who lives in the midst of nature and has still his senses.
– Thoreau's *Journal*, July 14, 1845

*E*merson has special talents unequalled.... In his world every man would be a poet, Love would reign, Beauty would take place, man and Nature would harmonize.

– Thoreau's *Journal*, 1845

Henry D Thoreau

*A*lmost any man knows how to earn money, but not one in a million knows how to spend it. If he had known as much as this he would never have earned it.

– Thoreau's *Journal*, 1846

Henry D Thoreau

*W*hen I am stimulated by reading the biographies of literary men to adopt some method of educating myself and directing my studies I can only resolve to keep unimpaired the freedom & wakefulness of my genius.

– Thoreau's *Journal*, December 1846

Henry D Thoreau

I confess that I have very little class spirit, and have almost forgotten that I ever spent four years at [Harvard]. That must have been in a former state of existence.

– From a letter to Henry Williams Jr., September 30, 1847

I do believe that the outward and the inward life correspond; that if any should succeed to live a higher life, others would not know of it, that difference and distance are one. To set about living a true life is to go on a journey to a distant country.
– From a letter to H. G. O. Blake, March 27, 1848

I do believe in simplicity. It is astonishing as well as sad, how many trivial affairs even the wisest man thinks he must attend to in a day.... So simplify the problems of life, distinguish the necessary and the real.
– From a letter to H. G. O. Blake, March 27, 1848

*B*ut one veil hangs over past, present and future, and it is the province of the historian to find out, not what was, but what is.
– *A Week on the Concord and Merrimack Rivers*, 1849

*T*he only danger in friendship is that it will end.
– *A Week on the Concord and Merrimack Rivers*, 1849

*T*here is more religion in men's science than
there is science in their religion.
– *A Week on the Concord and Merrimack Rivers,* 1849

Henry D Thoreau

*B*ut, to speak practically and as a citizen,
unlike those who call themselves no-government
men, I ask for, not at once no government, but at
once a better government. Let every man make
known what kind of government would
command his respect, and that will be one step
toward obtaining it.
– "Resistance to Civil Government," 1849

Henry D Thoreau

*I*f the injustice is part of the necessary friction of
the machine of government, let it go, let it go;
perchance it will wear smooth — certainly the
machine will wear out...but if it is of such a
nature that it requires you to be the agent of
injustice to another, then, I say, break the law.
Let your life be a counter friction to stop the
machine.
– "Resistance to Civil Government," 1849

What sort of fruit comes from living as if you were a-going to die? Live, rather, as if you were coming to life.

– Thoreau's *Journal*, 1849

Henry D. Thoreau

While my friend was my friend he flattered me, and I never heard the truth from him, but when he became my enemy he shot it to me on a poisoned arrow.... Hate is a good critic.

– Thoreau's *Journal*, 1849

Henry D. Thoreau

What after all does the practicalness [*sic*] of life amount to? The things immediately to be done are very trivial. I could postpone them all to hear the locust sing.

– *A Week on the Concord and Merrimack Rivers*, 1849

I do not prefer one religion or philosophy to another. I have no sympathy with the bigotry and ignorance which make...distinctions between one man's faith and another's — as Christians and heathens.... To the philosopher all sects, all nations are alike. I like Brahma, Hari, Buddha, the Great Spirit, as well as God.

– Thoreau's *Journal*, 1850

Henry D Thoreau

I think that I cannot preserve my health and spirits unless I spend four hours a day at least — and it is commonly more than that — sauntering through the woods and over the hills and fields absolutely free from all worldly engagements.... When sometimes I am reminded that the mechanics and shop-keepers stay in their shops not only all the forenoon, but all the afternoon too, sitting with crossed legs, so many of them — as if the legs were made to sit upon, and not to stand or walk upon — I think that they deserve some credit for not having all committed suicide long ago.

– "Walking," 1850

*M*an and his affairs, church and state — and school, trade and commerce, and manufactures and agriculture, — even politics, the most alarming of them all — I am pleased to see how little space they occupy in the landscape.
– "Walking," 1850

Henry D Thoreau

*W*hen we can no longer ramble in the fields of nature, we ramble in the fields of thought and literature. The old become readers. Our heads retain their strength when our legs have become weak.
– Thoreau's *Journal*, January 1, 1850

Henry D Thoreau

I love nature, I love the landscape, because it is so sincere. It never cheats me. It never jests. It is cheerfully, musically earnest.
– Thoreau's *Journal*, November 16, 1850

Henry D Thoreau

*H*owever mean your life is, meet it and live; do not shun it and call it hard names. It is not so bad as you are. It looks poorest when you are richest. The fault-finder will find faults even in paradise.
– Thoreau's *Journal*, October, 1850

The ocean is a wilderness reaching round the globe, wilder than a Bengal jungle and fuller of monsters.
– "An Excursion to Cape Cod," 1851

Henry D. Thoreau

If I have got false teeth, I trust that I have not got a false conscience. It is safer to employ the dentist than the priest — to repair the deficiencies of Nature.
– Thoreau's *Journal*, May 12, 1851

Henry D. Thoreau

Listen to music religiously, as if it were the last strain you might hear.
– Thoreau's *Journal*, June 12, 1851

Henry D. Thoreau

Ah, dear nature — the mere remembrance, after a short forgetfulness, of the pine woods! I come to it as a hungry man to a crust of bread.
– Thoreau's *Journal*, December 12, 1851

I fear that I have not got much to say about Canada, not having seen much; what I got by going to Canada was a cold.

– "An Excursion to Canada," 1852

Henry D. Thoreau

*T*he news I hear for the most part is not news to my genius. It is the stalest repetition.

– Thoreau's *Journal*, March 7, 1852

Henry D. Thoreau

*T*he bluebird carries the sky on his back.

– Thoreau's *Journal*, April 3, 1852

Henry D. Thoreau

*M*y nature may be still as this water — but it is not so pure & its reflections are not so distinct.

– Thoreau's *Journal*, April 11, 1852

Henry D. Thoreau

*O*ne man lies in his words and gets a bad reputation — another in his manners and enjoys a good one.

– Thoreau's *Journal*, June 25, 1852

*C*oncord is just as idiotic as ever in relation to the spirits and their knockings.... The hooting of owls — the croaking of frogs — is celestial wisdom in comparison.
– From a letter to Sophia Thoreau, July 13, 1852

Henry D. Thoreau

*M*an is continually saying to woman, Why will you not be more wise? Woman is continually saying to man, Why will you not be more loving? Unless each is both wise and loving, there can be neither wisdom nor love.
– From a letter to H. G. O. Blake, September, 1852

Henry D. Thoreau

*T*he fact is I am a mystic, a transcendentalist and a natural philosopher to boot.
– Thoreau's *Journal*, March 5, 1853

Henry D. Thoreau

*T*he wood thrush...touches a depth in me which no other bird's song does...a Shakespeare among birds.
– Thoreau's *Journal*, May 17, 1853

*N*ature is beautiful only as a place where life is to be lived. It is not beautiful to him who has not resolved on a beautiful life.
– Thoreau's *Journal*, July 21, 1853

Henry D Thoreau

*S*ometimes when I compare myself to other men, it seems as if I were more favored by the gods than they.
– *Walden*, 1854

Henry D Thoreau

I went to the woods because I wished to live deliberately, to front only the essential facts of life, and see if I could not learn what it had to teach, and not, when I came to die, discover that I had not lived.
– *Walden*, 1854

Henry D Thoreau

I learned this, at least, by my experiment: that if one advances confidently in the direction of his dreams, and endeavors to live the life which he has imagined, he will meet with a success unexpected in common hours.
– *Walden*, 1854

*I*t is not all books that are as dull as their readers.

– *Walden*, 1854

Henry D Thoreau

I wish my countrymen to consider, that whatever the human law may be, neither an individual nor a nation can ever commit the least act of injustice against the obscurest individual without having to pay the penalty for it. A government which deliberately enacts injustice, and persists in it, will at length ever become the laughing-stock of the world.

– "Slavery in Massachusetts," 1854

Henry D Thoreau

I bought me a spy-glass some weeks since. I buy but few things and those not till long after I begin to want them, so that when I do get them I am prepared to make a perfect use of them and extract their whole sweet.

– Thoreau's *Journal*, April 9, 1854

*T*he chief want is ever a life of deep experiences.

– Thoreau's *Journal*, June 8, 1854

Henry D. Thoreau

*T*hinking this afternoon of the prospect of my writing lectures...I realized how incomparably great the advantages of obscurity and poverty which I have enjoyed so long.

– Thoreau's *Journal*, September 19, 1854

Henry D. Thoreau

*A*fter lecturing twice this winter I feel that I am in danger of cheapening myself by trying to become a successful lecturer.... I would rather write books than lectures.

– Thoreau's *Journal*, December 6, 1854

Henry D. Thoreau

I hear faintly the cawing of a crow, far, far away... what a delicious sound! It is not merely crow calling to crow, for it speaks to me too.

– Thoreau's *Journal*, January 12, 1855

*K*nowledge does not come to us by details, but in flashes of light from heaven.
– "What Shall It Profit?," 1855

*P*erhaps I am more than usually jealous with respect to my freedom. I feel that my connection with, and obligation to, society are still very slight and transient.
– "What Shall It Profit?," 1855

*I*t is remarkable that among all the preachers there are so few moral teachers.
– "What Shall It Profit?," 1855

I do not know but it is too much to read one newspaper a week.
– "What Shall It Profit?," 1855

*D*o we call this the land of the free? What is it to be free from King George and continue the slaves of King Prejudice? What is it to be born free and not to live free? What is the value of any political freedom, but as a means to moral freedom?
– "What Shall It Profit?," 1855

Henry D. Thoreau

*V*ery few men take a wide survey. Their knowledge is very limited and particular.
– Thoreau's *Journal*, April 3, 1856

Henry D. Thoreau

*W*ading in the cold swamp braces me. I was invigorated, though I tasted not a berry.
– Thoreau's *Journal*, August 30, 1856

Henry D. Thoreau

*P*erhaps a more serious war is breaking out here. I seem to hear its distant mutterings.... There has not been anything which you could call union between North and South...for many years, and there cannot be so long as slavery is in the way.
– From a letter to Thomas Cholmondeley, October 20, 1856

*T*hat Walt Whitman of whom I wrote to you is the most interesting fact to me at present.... We ought to rejoice greatly in him.... He is awefully [*sic*] good.
– From a letter to H. G. O. Blake, December 7, 1856

Henry D. Thoreau

*I*n Wildness is the preservation of the world.
– "Walking," 1857

Henry D. Thoreau

*T*hat bobolink's song affected me as if we were endeavoring to keep down globes of melody within a vase full of liquid, but some bubbled up irrepressible.
– Thoreau's *Journal*, June 3, 1857

Henry D. Thoreau

*W*hen I hear music I fear no danger, I am invulnerable, I see no foe. I am related to the earliest times and to the latest.
– Thoreau's *Journal*, January 13, 1857

*T*ime never passes so quickly...as when I am engaged in composition, i.e. in writing down my thoughts. Clocks seem to have been put forward.
– Thoreau's *Journal*, January 27, 1858

Henry D. Thoreau

*W*hat great interval is there between him who is caught in Africa and made a plantation slave of in the south, and him who is caught in New England and made a Unitarian minister of?
– Thoreau's *Journal*, February 28, 1857

Henry D. Thoreau

*T*he scarlet oak leaf! What a graceful and pleasing outline! If I were a drawing master, I would set my pupils to copying these leaves.
– Thoreau's *Journal*, November 11, 1858

Henry D. Thoreau

*H*ow full of soft, pure light the western sky now, after sunset! I love to see the outlines of the pines against it.
– Thoreau's *Journal*, December 12, 1858

I perceive that we partially die ourselves through sympathy at the death of each of our friends or near relatives. Each such experience is an assault on our vital force.
– Thoreau's *Journal*, February 3, 1859

*O*ctober is the month of painted leaves.
– "Autumnal Tints," March 1859

A great part of our troubles are literally domestic or originate in the house and from being indoors. I could write an essay entitled "Out of Doors" [and] undertake a crusade against houses.
– Thoreau's *Journal*, April 26, 1859

A man of rare common sense and directness of speech, as of action, a transcendentalist above all, a man of ideas and principles, that was what distinguished him. Not yielding to a whim or transient impulse, but carrying out the purpose of a life.
– "A Plea for Captain John Brown," 1859

I do not believe in erecting statues to those who still live in our hearts, whose bones have not yet crumbled in the earth around us, but I would rather see the statue of Captain Brown in the Massachusetts State-House yard, than that of any other man whom I know. I rejoice that I live in this age, that I am his contemporary.
– "A Plea for Captain John Brown," 1859

Some eighteen hundred years ago Christ was crucified, this morning, perchance, Captain Brown was hung. These are the two ends of a chain which is not without its links. He is not Old Brown any longer, he is an angel of light.
– "A Plea for Captain John Brown," 1859

You are expected to do your duty, not in spite of everything but one, but in spite of everything.
– Thoreau's *Journal*, September 24, 1859

I feel very ignorant, of course, in a museum. I know nothing about the things they have there — no more than I would know about my friends in the tomb.
– Thoreau's *Journal*, February 18, 1860

Henry D. Thoreau

*A*lmost all wild apples are handsome. They cannot be too gnarly and crabbed and rusty to look at. The gnarliest will have some redeeming traits even to the eye.
– "Wild Apples," February 14, 1860

Henry D. Thoreau

*S*o we saunter toward the Holy Land, till one day the sun shall shine more brightly than ever he has done, shall perchance shine into our minds and hearts, and light up our whole lives with a great awakening light, so warm and serene and golden as on a bank-side in Autumn.
– "Walking," September 9, 1860

So some, it seems to me, elect their leaders for their crookedness. But I think that a straight stick makes the best cane and an upright man the best ruler.

– "An Address on the Succession of Forest Trees,"
  September 9, 1860

Henry D. Thoreau

Although I do not believe that a plant will spring up where no seed has been, I have great faith in a seed. Convince me that you have a seed there and I am prepared to expect miracles.

– "An Address on the Succession of Forest Trees,"
  September 9, 1860

Henry D. Thoreau

Every man is entitled to come to Cattle-shows, even a transcendentalist; and for my part I am more interested in the men than the cattle.

– "An Address on the Succession of Forest Trees,"
  September 20, 1860

Henry D. Thoreau

Pears, it is truly said, are less poetic than apples. They have neither the beauty nor the fragrance of apples, but their excellence is in their flavor, which speaks to a grosser sense.

– Thoreau's *Journal*, October 11, 1860

W̶hat sort of cultivation, or civilization...is ours to boast of...if we leave the land poorer than we found it?
– Thoreau's *Journal*, November 10, 1860

Henry D. Thoreau

T̶alk about slavery! It is not the peculiar institution to the South! It exists wherever men are bought and sold, wherever a man allows himself to be made a tool and surrenders his inalienable rights of reason and conscience.
– Thoreau's *Journal*, December 4, 1860

Henry D. Thoreau

W̶herever men have lived there is a story to be told, and it depends chiefly on the story-teller or historian whether that is interesting or not.
– Thoreau's *Journal*, March 18, 1861

Henry D. Thoreau

B̶lessed are they who never read a newspaper, for they shall see Nature, and through her, God.
– From a letter to Parker Pillsbury, April 10, 1861

Henry D. Thoreau.